Danny Draws

by Holly Harper
illustrated by Ana Sebastián

Teta was going out.

"Emmy is coming to look after you," said Teta.

Danny's tummy was twisty. He had not yet met Emmy.

"It's nice to meet you," said Emmy.
"Do you like bugs?"

“I love bugs!” Danny said excitedly.

Emmy showed Danny her notebook.

“You are really good at art. Could you teach me to paint?” Danny asked.

Emmy smiled.

Emmy drew a small, spotty bug.

Danny painted it red and black.

“It looks like it’s alive!” said Danny.

The bug suddenly flew out of the notebook. It landed on Emmy's head.

Danny was confused but Emmy just smiled.

"Art is so *exciting!*" said Emmy.

Bugs crawled out of the notebook.

“This yellow one is so cute!” said Emmy.

A red and blue bird flew out.

"I think it's hungry," said Danny.

Next a possum jumped right out of the notebook. It ran at the red and blue bird.

"Oh no, look out!" Danny shouted.

The bird tipped the cup of water. Danny's shirt got all soggy.

Then a kangaroo launched into the air.

The possum dived under a chair.

"It's like a circus!" said Danny. "The whole place is a mess!"

"Teta will be back home soon. How are we going to fix this?" asked Danny.

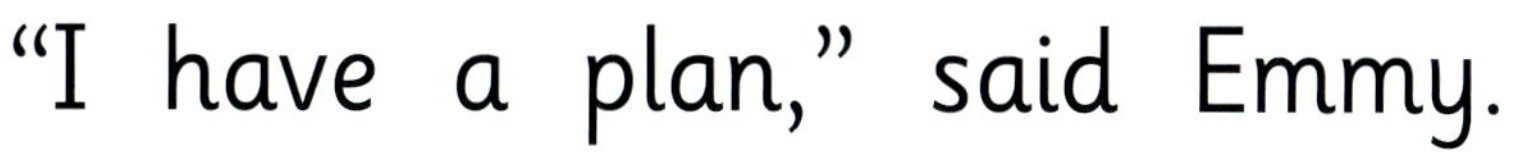

"I have a plan," said Emmy.

She flipped the notebook to a new sheet.

"Let's draw a place that they might like to go," Emmy said.

They drew a forest.

"Let's see who wants to visit our forest," Emmy said excitedly.

The bugs popped back into the notebook.

The bird flew down from its perch.

The possum came out from under the chair.

"I think that's all of them," said Danny. "We need to clean this mess up."

"Quick! Teta is home!" said Emmy.

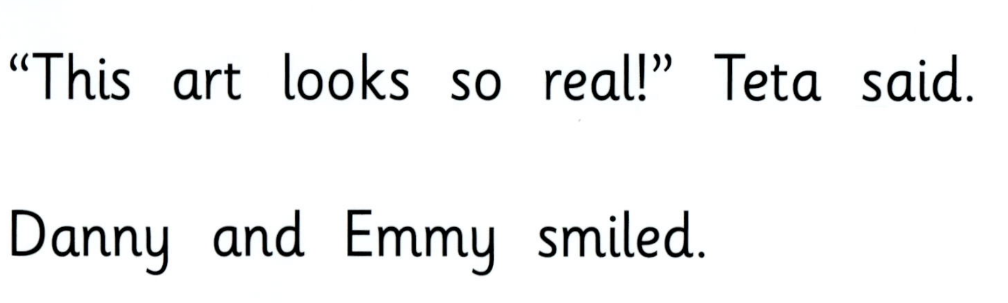

"This art looks so real!" Teta said.

Danny and Emmy smiled.

“Who is this?” Teta asked.

“I’m not sure,” Danny giggled.

Look Back

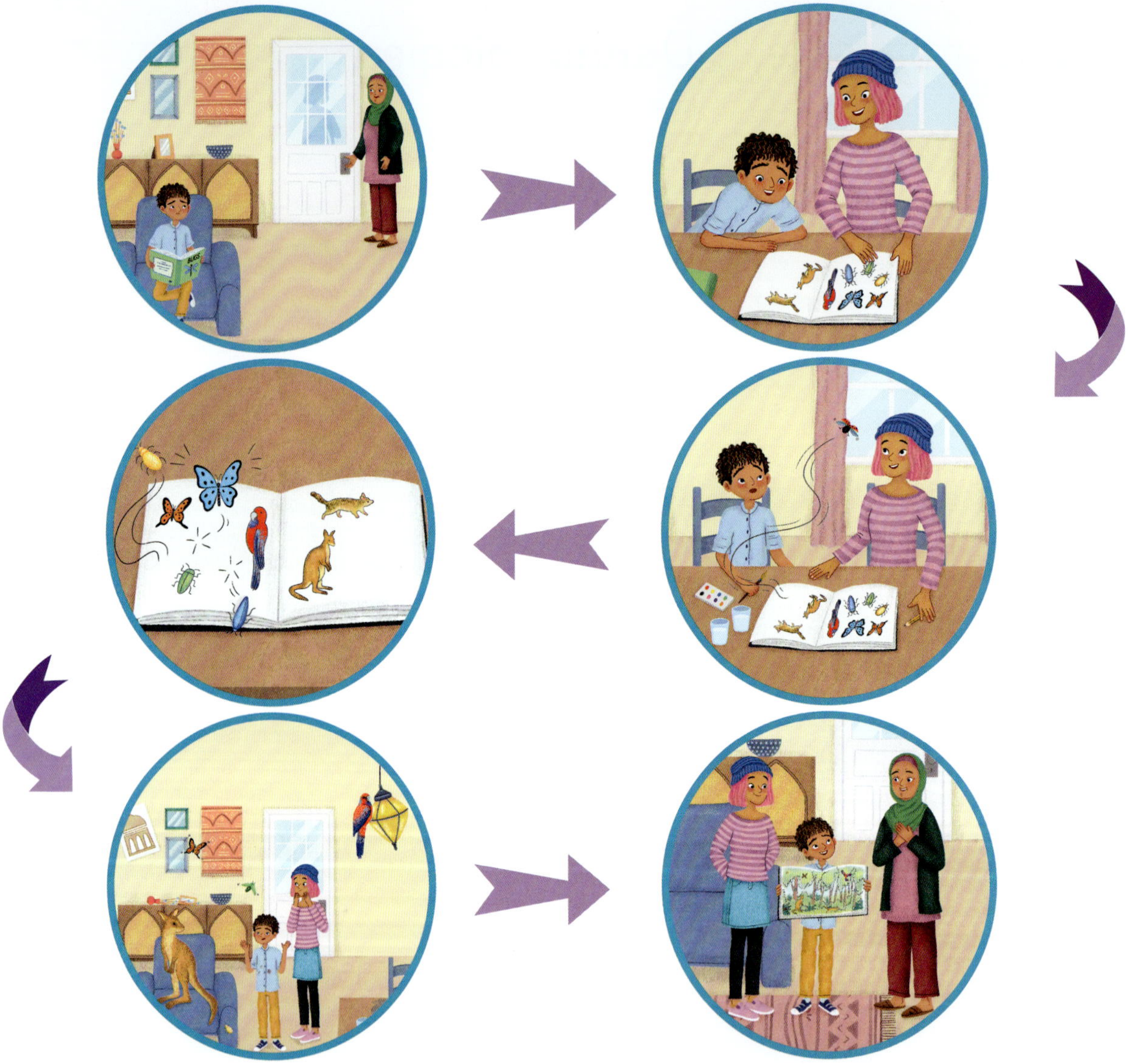

Encourage students to use the pictures to retell the story.